# *My Stroke, Soul Survivor*

Lisa Smith

Copyright 2025 Lisa Smith

All rights reserved.

No part of this publication shall be reproduced, transmitted, or sold in whole or in part in any form without prior written consent of the author, except as provided by the United States of American copyright law. Any unauthorized usage of the text without express written permission of the publisher is a violation of the author's copyright and is illegal and punishable by law. All trademarks appearing in this guide are the property of their owner.

The opinions expressed by the Author are not necessarily those held by Publishers.

The information contained within this book is strictly for informational purposes. As such, the Author and Publisher do not assume responsibility for websites (or their content) that are not owned by the publisher. Readers are advised to do their own due diligence when it comes to making decisions.

*For my family and friends and fairies*

# *Table of Contents*

### *Memoir* .................................................................... 3

- Who Knew? ........................................................ 6
- Before the Fall .................................................... 9
- Summons from Fate .......................................... 12
- Hole in my Heart ............................................... 15
- The Stroke ......................................................... 23
- The Fairies ......................................................... 27
- The Diagnosis .................................................... 31
- A Whisper of Hope ............................................ 33
- New Beginning .................................................. 35
- Coming Home ................................................... 39

### *In Praise of Your Aphasia* ................................... 47

- For Lisa ............................................................. 48
- Falling ............................................................... 50
- Inscrutability ..................................................... 51
- Mark's Interview ............................................... 52
- Teaching a Class ................................................ 54
- The Art of Falling .............................................. 57
- One Art ............................................................. 59

> Two Art or Aphasia ............................................... 61

The Power of Forgetting ............................................. 63

Words Like Water ..................................................... 65

> High Brow ............................................................ 68

Oh, The Pearls! ........................................................ 70

Grief ...................................................................... 73

Gyrokinetic Exercise ................................................. 77

## *Poetry* .............................................................. *81*

When I Was a Tiny One or The Stroke Survivor .......... 82

A Brand New World Opens Before Me ..................... 83

Numb .................................................................... 84

Two Birds and One Aphasia .................................... 86

What Are You Reading Right Now ........................... 87

Falling ................................................................... 88

Oubaitori ............................................................... 89

Boredom ............................................................... 90

Two in Thirds ........................................................ 91

Inscrutability ......................................................... 92

Oh, Silent Night ..................................................... 93

It's Christmas Time ................................................ 94

Fireworks Inside of Me ........................................... 95

Two Art or a Stroke ................................................ 96

I'm Weepy Now ..................................................... 98

Our Dog and I, We Are a Pair! ................................. 99

Justice ................................................................. 101

Oh, Melinda ......................................................... 102

Theft ..................................................................... 103
Beautiful Toes ....................................................... 104
A Baby's Wonder .................................................. 105
A Song .................................................................. 106
Misunderstanding ................................................ 107
A New Beginning ................................................. 108
And So, We Shall Rise, Fall and Rise .................. 109
Hear! Hear! The Caregivers! ................................ 110

## 1998 Poems ........................................................... 112

Vintage ................................................................. 113
My Children and the Sea ..................................... 114
5BDR, 4BA + MAID'S ........................................ 116
Hard and Bitter as a Rusted Nail ......................... 117
The World is so Beautiful, I Must be Dying ....... 118
Mercy .................................................................... 119
Legacy ................................................................... 120
I Dreamed We Were Young ................................ 121
Etruscan ............................................................... 122
Spanish Dancing .................................................. 123
Vacation for Stanley Hall .................................... 124

About the Author ..................................................... 126

# *At the Student Poetry Reading*

*I guess you could call me broken,*
says one. *I'm still lonely,* says another,
*but now I can name it with a song.*

*In my poem,* says another,
*I can forget I am forgotten. Now
I understand being misunderstood,*

says another. And another says,
in a bold, undeniable voice of power,
*I won't step down from myself again.*

And they are beautiful, beautiful,
standing one by one at the mic where
they have come forth at last from
behind the curtain.

Poem copyright 2021 by Kim Stafford,
                              from *Poetry* (March 2021)
Reprinted by permission of Kim Stafford.

# Memoir

I'm a helper. There I said it. Seventy-years-old and I'm just now getting this, I'm a helper. I wanted to be a star, to be an actress or a dancer. But I am a teacher and helper. A teacher likes to give (and give a lot) to the "students" wherever they may be. I learned a few things since my stroke, and now I'm going to teach it to you. I want this book to inspire you, to enlighten you. I want to try to help those with stroke and brain injury. I want to help the caregivers. I want to help you and myself by writing, by speaking from the heart.

--- *Lisa Smith*

*Explaining the count of a ballet step*

## *Who Knew?*

Who knew? When one had the power, one had the intelligence, the savvy, the lived experience. I knew it when I had it, I felt it. I saved photographs, newspaper clippings, cards, the boys' Crayola drawings, and reams of dog-eared papers I had written. I knew it.

I am Lisa Smith; I was a dance teacher and professor for most of my life. Hard to believe I am 71 years old now, but I am not through yet. I decided a stroke wasn't going to hold me back.

I want to try old things like swimming and the Pilates reformer. I still want to write poems. I want to find out what I can do in a class setting with stroke and brain injury. As far as I am concerned, the sky's the limit--and why not?

Wait a minute! It was hard, miserable, and heartbreaking. The body that once moved freely betrayed me; the mind that once choreographed lessons now stumbled over words.

I was a professor and teacher of ballet and modern dance, World Dance, and Pedagogy at the University of Texas, El Paso (UTEP) for 20 years. Before that, I earned an MFA degree in creative writing at UTEP. And before that I was a dancer and danced and directed my way through Texas and Switzerland.

And I had a stroke!

*Showing the dancer how to turn*

## *Before the Fall*

I was tired. This was to be the last year, or two years, of my teaching with the students. The last year, or two years, of putting on a show. And the first time I would manage the American College Dance Association (ACDA) conference. It was my opportunity to UTEP and the beauty of El Paso--the west Texas city where I raised my children and taught my students. Over the years, the students have become high school dance teachers, college dance instructors, studio teachers or directors, educators, performers in Broadway shows and other stage events, stage managers, lighting designers—so many paths.

I saw my own two sons in them too – young men stepping their way into a world full of unknown. I wanted to shield them, both the young men and the students. I wanted to show them how to dance through it anyway.

They had a good life spread out before them, paths their parents helped shape, or that they would choose for themselves. And I was the steward to guide them through the bumps and rough patches. Not just in dance, but in life.

They could choose their path, Ballet, Math, English, History, or any other subject. I had studied Anthropology and Ballet, and darned if my life wasn't about these two subjects!

What I'm trying to say is, "the world is an oyster." You can do anything you wish or go anywhere you would like to go because you have the ability to do so much! But ballet is hard. It's got all the bumps, ups and downs, and rough patches going on. And there are cuts and bruises and mirrors staring back at you with legs or bodies that are too thin, too fat, too small, or too long! You are the instrument. You don't get to leave the textbook behind. You *are* the book. Your body and your mind become the message. You are the "means of expression," to make the audience feel something positive, something painful, something out of this world.

Twenty years felt like enough. I had counseled students, administered the program, creating curricula, recruiting, budgeting, advocating for the dance programs, teaching, and choreographing. I had a lot of help from all my colleagues over the years. Myron Nadel—may he rest in peace—was there from the beginning teaching Ballet and Jazz. Through the years, wonderful teachers taught Modern Dance, World Dance, Dance Appreciation. Still, I was the glue for the students, the teachers, the administration, and the University. The string, trying to tie up every little thing.

I had given so much to the city, to UTEP, and it would shape me in return. But in that year, or two, there were still performances to plan, visions unexpressed, projects waiting. I didn't know it yet, but I was already falling.

## *Summons from Fate*

I was 66 years old when I had a stroke. This was in the middle of a crisis, at least for me. I had been organizing a major event for dancers and educators from all over Texas and New Mexico, plus other states, juggling logistics, politics, and an avalanche of to-do. That mounting pressure might not have caused the stroke, but it certainly set the stage for my body's quiet, catastrophic protest.

I and other faculty were summoned to the office of the chair. The chairwoman had the floor, which was good because I couldn't think of one thing to say. Not one! But this project had been mine, the chairwoman and I had been scrabbling over details.

Amid all the talk of budget, names, and universities and I sat silently, unable to contribute. All the university teachers were fluttering about the details: "But what about the fees and charges? What about the rates? Texas State or the University of Texas? Clark, Fullerton, Harding? No, Harding, Rinelli, Clark, and Sanchez." Little bits of Post-it notes, like confetti, were stuck on the chair's window looking outward to El Paso and Juarez. Everyone seemed to be in motion, except for me. I couldn't hold on to the details.

My head began to swim, faced with big notebooks of names and dates I somehow no longer recognized. I didn't make a sound. I knew what Texas State was, my son had gone there. And I knew The University of Texas at Austin; both my husband, Mark, and I went to school there. So why did everything feel foreign? *Maybe I'm just tired,* I thought.

I went out to dinner with my colleagues and then drove home and went immediately to work on my laptop at my desk. I felt just fine. Eventually, I went to bed. *It was sweet, my bed,* I thought, and went to sleep. Mark had already gone to sleep.

Sometime during the night, I fell. I was still half asleep when I hit the floor. Mark woke up and found me—vomit on the floor, the dog licking it up. He asked, "Are you getting up?" And I said, "No, no, no," but I meant to say YES! Later, he told me he thought it was food poisoning, so called the women I had had dinner with. I don't remember much after that. I lay with my head on the floor, and then--I blacked out.

*I've heard this from many stroke survivors, that their words often get mixed up. We know what we want to say, but it all comes out wrong. I didn't exhibit the classic telltale signs of a stroke—at least not at first. No balance issues, no loss of vision, no face drooping, arm weakness, or slurred speech. But I did have general weaknesses and disorientation. And I was confused and fatigued. The balance issues, face drooping, arm weakness and speech problems came later.

It would seem the B.E.F.A.S.T. stroke signs (Balance, Eyes, Facial drooping, Arms, Time) are more typical for men. I'm glad to see that more classic heart failure or stroke signs for women are now coming to the forefront, or, at least, are in the running!

## *Hole in my Heart*

Long before the stroke, I had already learned how to survive. When I was 16, I underwent heart surgery for a congenital defect. I had a "hole in my heart," and Dr. Cooley, the legendary surgeon, patched me up. That early wound stayed with me. I didn't know that one day I would face another rupture, this time in my brain. But I already knew how to heal.

Dr. Cooley was a cardiothoracic surgeon famous for implanting one of the first artificial hearts, and he was renowned for the first successful human heart transplant. I did not have one of the artificial hearts or human hearts, but Texas Children's Hospital in Houston in 1969 had a lot of patients, both adults and children, with various heart diseases and defects. For instance, I knew a 21- year-old woman with Raynaud's Syndrome and a heart defect, and a boy who had a heart that worked backwards. Right down the hall, a new male patient had an artificial heart! These cases surrounded me, making me feel both vulnerable and in awe of the science that would save us.

I remained fascinated and curious, even when I got to the cardiac imaging room. I don't remember his name—just that he was young, maybe 30, and sweating as he tried to insert the needle into my groin artery. I was sweating too. Other Doctors crowded around us. He got the needle in, but I could hear the Doctors sighing in the room. He was about 30, most of the doctors were around 30 to 40, and would troop in behind Dr. Cooley, pens and notebooks in their hands, ready to jot down any significance announcement. But in that moment, it was me, a terrified teenager and an embarrassed doctor.

It was time for the surgery. My sedative was good, but I still remember the yellow shift style dress my mom put on. I picked it out, that and the olive-green swing dress, and she wore it just for me. And there was Dad and my brother, Doug. The "little" girls, Sally and Cookie, were still at our grandparents' house in Yoakum, Texas.

I woke up in the ICU. My arms were tied down, but I could still move my hands, and I was surprised I didn't feel Frankenstein-like stitches down my stomach and sternum. *Oh, shoot, I've woken up before the surgery,* I thought. Then a black angel, a nurse, said, "The operation was a success. You're done cured!" Dr. Cooley did a nice thing. He made the incision horizontal, below my breasts, instead of up and down!

I remember the shriek of the 12-year-old boy who was lying right next to me. The nurse had removed his drainage tube. I looked down, I had two drainage tubes! Damn! It was like being stabbed from the inside out and the hole was sutured by thread, twice.

But the pain of heart surgery? It's all a blur, but I can remember that it hurt, when coughing, when just sitting up, and I couldn't raise my arms above 45 degrees. And the fatigue, my heavy chest, the smells of antiseptic, disinfectant, and blood.

I had a heart murmur, an unusual sound, and it was the mitral valve stenosis and regurgitation, a hole in my heart. The system should flow smoothly, but because the mitral valve never formed properly, it didn't. I was hooked up to the heart and lung machine, the doctors cracked the sternum open and went to work in the left atrium and the lower left ventricle. Dr.

Cooley placed a patch made of Dacron, a type of synthetic polyester, into the hole in my heart.

I woke up in my room at night and there was Dr. Cooley at the foot of my bed, alone and calm, "How are we doing, Hon?" I'd never seen him without the other good doctors around, but here he was, in the flesh all alone!

Back in Dallas after my surgery, Dr. Bashour, a cardiologist, told me that I was good to go and that I would live a good life. And I did live a good life, as a wife and a mother and a professional.

My father wouldn't let me strain myself during the fall of the next year. But as a high school junior, I wouldn't let go of the drill team. In Texas, land of the Friday night lights, football was king. And for the girls, drill team was everything. Besides, I had something to prove—to myself and everyone who saw me as fragile. At half time when the drill team marched out on the field, I was alone in the stands, dressed in my Caballeros uniform. White gloves, orange and white gauntlets, vest and short skirt all fringed with Naugahyde, and a cowgirl hat. I got to be square in the middle, watching the Caballeros marching and kicking down the field. I put aside a lot of my frustrations in high school the last two years, but I stood tall and was known as the "girl who had a hole in her heart." Even though I didn't march on the field my junior year, I did make officer the next year.

Little did Dr. Bashour and I know that at the age of 66, I would be at St. David's Medical Center in Austin, Texas to have an ablation procedure where the doctors would electrically "zap" various area in my heart that were triggering an irregular heartbeat.

El Paso Cardiology Associates was where I learned of cardiac ablation and AFib. I didn't know I had AFib, but there were many times during my adult life when I knew something wasn't right. Like when I was 19 and studying anthropology at the University of Texas in Austin, Texas. I drove to the Zuni Pueblo in northern New Mexico with a high school friend. But before we made it to the Reservation on top of the mesa, I insisted we turn around and go back to Austin. My heart was feeling very stressed.

Or when I was 21 and my mother died. Broken again, this time through the inside out.

Everybody, not just me, was devasted.

And again at 36, when I was a mother myself of two little boys. This time I went to the doctor, but now my heart had stopped jumping around. He listened to my heart, gave me a stress test, and put on a cardiac monitor, but to no avail.

And at 45 when I was at rehearsal. Confused about the sensations, I borrowed a yoga anatomy book from a friend to try and figure out what was going on. I found the rib cage with all the bone structure and cartilage and decided the heart must have had something to do with my Costochondral joint. Maybe that was it. But none of those instances were like what I was experiencing in 2019 when cardiac ablation was recommended.

***

Mark and I sat in a pre-op waiting area at St. David's hospital in Austin an entire morning, afternoon, and evening. Finally, at 7pm that night, they took me in for what turned out to be a three-hour long operation involving 52 different sites! I was exhausted. I had gone all day and night without food or water. I was allowed to have some shaved ice. The next morning, Dr. Horton and his staff started me on Xarelto (Rivaroxaban), which thins your blood, so it takes longer to clot.

The thing about taking Xarelto is, once you start, you can't miss two doses, or more. I'll never know what happened. With all the stress of the ACDA conference looming, did I forget to take it? Or did the Xarelto simply fail to do its job? The bloodwork after my stroke showed I had the correct levels of the drug in my body. But who knows. What's done is done. Now, I've got to focus on what happens in the aftermath of my stroke.

Mark and I thought we had come through the worst of it after the ablation procedure. We just felt it was all over and done, finished. The warning on the Xarelto packaging states, "It can treat and prevent blood clots" and "may lower the risk of stroke." Notice how it says "can" and "may"? I skimmed through that part of the WARNING. Five and a half months later, I had the stroke.

I wish I had opted for the WATCHMAN procedure, a small parachute-shaped implant which was designed to block off the heart where the clots typically form in patients with AFib. It acts like a tiny filter. Maybe the clot that caused my stroke wouldn't have formed. I had a stroke in January 2020. The WATCHMAN was FDA-approved in 2015, but no one ever mentioned it to me or Mark until it was too late. Why did the doctors not tell us about the WATCHMAN device before I had my heart ablation?

*My brain after the stroke; the white section is the damaged area*

*My brain (2)*

# *The Stroke*

> "Dr. Payne had been summoned by the hospital, as he was our primary care provider. After some discussion with the doctors at the hospital, he told me that it appeared Lisa would never walk or talk again, given the size of the affected area in her brain."
>
> *-Mark Bandy*

Thus, the waiting game began. Poor Mark, and poor me. Mark, bewildered and shocked, and for me, trapped in a body that no longer obeyed. Though I couldn't speak or move much, my mind was beginning to take in the strange new world around me.

There are two things, I remember, from my first stay after my stroke:

One -- A loud siren and a bumpy ride, and the next thing I knew, I was in the hospital, which one, I didn't know. I woke up that day to an older nurse fixing my hair on the right side in some kind of hair roller and fitting me with a bonnet. I thought that was kind of dumb, a *bonnet*? The head cover matched my gown. Complete with a bow and lace trim. I looked down at my gown, and my ...*wheelchair?* So, some kind of hair roller, my bonnet, matching gown, with three ties to the back side, and a wheelchair! What happened to me? I lost consciousness.

Two – the second night was pretty awful. I tossed and turned, and I couldn't sleep. *My life was a mess, a god-awful mess,* I thought. *How can you teach?* My speech was non-existent, my arm and leg non-functioning, and my face drooped on one side. My identity dissolving!

My husband snores when he sleeps, often very loudly. It was crowded in my hospital room, and he was right next to me. I called out to him many times, but it was no use; me, with garbled speech, and he with his droning snores. The room was stuffy, my sheets were uncomfortable, and it was noisy. My room was next to the main station where the intercom call button had been placed. "Dr. Ortiz, Dr. Ortiz, come to the waiting area," "Medivac, medivac," "Dr. He, Dr. He stat, Dr. He."

I decided, or my brain decided, let's see if I can turn around and I probably would sleep better. I got somewhere in the middle of my bed. The bed rail was up, and my head rested on the one bed rail, and my tail and leg on the other. My leg and arm would not cooperate! I waited and waited for my nurse to come in. Surely, someone would come in to help me! Two of the nurses came into my room, and the young female gasped when she saw me. The male, after he untangled me, proceeded to tell the young female nurse, nonchalantly, "Get the sheets. No one will know."

But I knew. I couldn't speak, but I knew. My sometime brain had apparently packed a suitcase and gone on holiday—without notice. This was ridiculous. I was ridiculous. Can you imagine, directing a dance with a brain/language disorder, with a non-dominant hand, and my right arm and leg on the fritz. I was crushed, devastated, and I wanted to scream, but I knew that I could trust my friend and confidante, my "angel" or the Lilac Fairy of Wisdom (a part I had played on stage), and this is how I thought of my adult-self.

In Switzerland, we did a production of West Side Story, the Leonard Bernstein and Steven Sondheim musical featuring a song entitled, "Cool" (Stay cool, Boy!). In German, the refrain was "Bleib kühl," (snap! snap!) For some reason, the words came back to me in that moment. My adult-self told me to *bleib kühl, (stay cool),* even though I wanted to cry or yell. But this is what calmed me down. When I was nervous or panicky I thought about that number, "Cool." It even made me smile!

\*\*\*

Cookie and Sally, my sisters, remember other things from my time in the hospital. Cookie had noticed, for instance, that a doctor at the front desk was the spitting image of Peter Lorre, the 1940s film actor. When I was out of my room and passed by the front desk, I saw that he indeed resembled Peter Lorre!

I looked at Cookie, nodded my head, and furrowed my brow as if to say "Oh, yeah!" At least my brain was tracking when it came to creepy 1940s movie stars! But Cookie said, "I told the doctors you understand *everything*!"

Sally remembers that we were at the throat x-ray machine waiting for the technician, and she had an idea. She would sing the "Supercalifragilisticexpialidocious" (hard isn't it!) song from "Mary Poppins." She sang a line, and I would parrot it back to her. Pretty soon I got the hang of it, so we sang all the tunes from musicals to the amusement of the medics. When I returned home, I would sing and watch the musicals on the TV! My younger son likes to watch "Seven Brides for Seven Brothers," and I like "The King and I," and we both liked "West Side Story." Tracking on musicals from the 50s and 60s, as well.

Those early days in the hospital were foggy, messy, and sometimes absurd. But amid the confusion, I felt safe, and I caught glimpses of myself through music and movies, through my sisters' love, through Mark and the boy's love, and through moments of humor!

## *The Fairies*

If you have a stroke, make sure you have lots of friends and family. I had my closest guys-- my husband and two boys--and I love them dearly. They all have a good sense of humor! But when it came to the girls--sisters, cousins, and friends--I am beholden to them. One by one they came from around the country, from Alaska and Vero Beach, Virginia and Los Angeles, Dallas and Oakland, and of course, El Paso. They came and delivered! Sitting and sleeping by my side, reassuring, and encouraging me. Reminding me of who I was.

In 1985, I danced in Sleeping Beauty with the Austin Ballet Theatre, in the Lilac Fairy role I mentioned earlier. But after my stroke, I played the part of Sleeping Beauty! I was sleeping like a baby beauty, maybe not so "beautiful" and maybe not so "sleeping-ful," but I did sleep for two and a half days in the house, and a day and a half in the hospital. But never mind! The Fairies gave all the gifts to the baby, who would grow up and become the Sleeping Beauty. Grace, joy, a musical voice, a serene temperament, honesty and courage. That is The Sleeping Beauty, but the girls did much to help me to understand, in a graceful way, my new situation. To laugh, to use my singing voice, and to maintain a serene temperament, along with courage and joy.

One word about dancing and song therapy. I am a great believer in Art Therapy. So long as you find that little bit of dancing, or art, or musicality, perhaps if you can whistle or hum, you will find a step, a note or a phrase that lifts you up, that frees you.

***

After a few days in intensive care, I got a new room farther away from the main station. But it was still very hectic. There were the doctors: Neurologists, Cardiologists, Endocrinologists, Hematologists (hospitals sure have a lot of "ologists"). The nurses: one for the pills twice a day, and one periodically to see if I needed anything. The Phlebotomist twice a day (I felt like a pin cushion!), and Radiology for the arm (2x), and head (3x). Then there was physical therapy, speech therapy, administration, friends, sisters, family, and I was the star of the show!

I did manage to figure out which hospital I was at. And I did venture out from my room, and floor, up to the cafeteria and down to the first floor where the gift shop was, and out through the front door. I recognized the building but not the inside, and not the view of the mountains, or downtown. It was the same hospital where my boys were born, Sierra Medical Center. Now it was the "Hospitals of Providence Sierra

Campus," hospital for heart care, neuro, and brain services, as well as back and spine surgeries.

As a choreographer at heart, I spent entire days casting my imaginary ballet. It was a way to stay connected to who I was—and who I still am. I'd watch the hallway, the cafeteria, the physical therapy, choosing which patients or hospital workers would be in my next production. I was looking for which one would be the supporting one and which one would be the lifted one, a "hospital pas de deux." I chose a fit man in a wheelchair who had a foot cut off and the petite physical therapy woman. I chose three chorus line dancers, two female nurses, and one male, an orderly, who would dance and sing.

Call it boredom, but in those endless hours my mind turned back to the stage, and they were my challenged fantasy dancers. My plan, when I got out of the hospital, was to take some of the patients, medics, and physical therapists back to the UTEP Theatre and do a little benefit for the hospital and stroke victims. I was thinking and planning right there!

*Greg Easley (The Prince) and I in the second act, looking for Sleeping Beauty*

## *The Diagnosis*

In the middle of the night, the door opened. The orderly entered and said, "Arm x-ray." Without further explanation, he unplugged the monitors from my bed and wheeled me out--fast! We passed through a maze of little doors, big doors, into an elevator, down to the first floor, and around the corner to even more doors. The hallways were deserted. It was eerie, and I had to wonder, *why now? What were they doing in the middle of the night?* Something about this felt serious—not that the speech issues and paralyzed leg weren't—but this was different. My arm must have been worse than I realized.

In the X-ray, everyone was cheerful and brisk. I was transferred out of my bed and into the X-ray bed, and back into my bed. The female medic said, as she positioned the X-ray film, smiling all the while, "The humerus is separated from the bone, the scapula. When the muscles in the shoulder are weak, gravity is enough to pull the humerus out of the shoulder socket." It was a *subluxation* of my humerus.

My arm, humerus, was separated from the shoulder bone, the scapula? I know when I did this. At home, when I got out of bed the night of my stroke, I fell on my right side. I scooted up, I don't know why, but I had the urgency of *"I've got to stand up now."*

Yes, this was serious. I stared at the X-ray--my arm, my humerus—disconnected and drifting, like it had been unmoored from my body. It looked lonely. Severed and alone out in the voids without a tether of the shoulder. How could something so essential just slip away? Then I looked at her, still smiling. The orderly had turned the bed around and away we went. I crumbled and I wanted to cry. How could I teach? This was too much. *Bleib kühl,* Lisa, "stay cool."

Oh, but I wanted to cry and yell! The orderly just left me there in the room, he turned the lights out and was gone. I was alone, with the time to think and stew. This was bad! I couldn't stop thinking about it. Would I be in a wheelchair, my right arm and hand limp, and my speech illogical and scattered? This was the first time I ever thought, really thought about it. I had been blind about my situation. I was trying not to think about it. I was trying to do my best, but like one of Scarlett O'Hara's many quips in *Gone with the Wind*, "I'd think about it tomorrow." But this was awful!

# *A Whisper of Hope*

Amidst the confusion and despair, an inner voice--call it my friend and confidante, my angel or Lilac Fairy of Wisdom--gave me the proper lecture, *now let's see what you can do about this.* I cannot say if it was the ballet training or my experience as a teacher or just plain hard work, but it sparked my determination and journey of self-discovery. From the tiniest seed planted somewhere in my brain, my mind was leaning toward optimism. So, what if my arm doesn't work? Let's see about the leg and speech problems.

I had to figure out what was causing that speech deficiency, so I studied and practiced my phonetics and writing skills at NeuroRestorative, the longer-term rehab facility I went to after I was released from the hospital. It was two-fold; I couldn't say anything and remembered half of nothing. I could remember the names and faces of people, places, things, close to me, or the acts to me or other people, but I couldn't clearly enunciate, producing just a garbled sound. I could read and say, for instance, a "handbag" or "comb." I knew the handbag, could see the handbag, could read the "HANDBAG," but I don't even know what I said. Could be "handbag," could be something else.

And I remember pretty much everything, or at least I used to. But just as the word or phrase would come up, a wall of fog would loom inside my brain. I was stumped and stunned in the last remnant of the fog. The word or the phrase wouldn't come up! I couldn't produce the word that came into view, and so, I didn't make the effort. This has been a thing since the stroke in 2020, but I know it will be gone if I just work on it. Already the wall is beginning to crumble.

Now the leg: I was scared. Too scared to go along without a wheelchair, walker, a pole, a barre, bed, dresser or table. No siree! I could stand up, but that's about it. Fear is a sneaky fellow. Anxiety, procrastination, depression--little by little I became more afraid. *Not so scared, in the early 1980s, when I leaped across the ballet room, jumped up and landed in my partner's hands in a 'fish' dive, or perched up on top of my partner's shoulders,* I thought. Right up until the stroke, I was uneasy and unwilling to try anything that involved jumps or balance without a barre or table, from one leg on the ground and the other leg at 45 - 50 degrees. After all, I am 71! But now I am dizzy and a little afraid. I don't feel anything but lack of feeling in my right buttock, and my whole right leg is sluggish. Nothing from my right heel, and my right toes curl downwards and inwards. My hip, thigh, knee, calf, and ankle and thereabouts are impaired by "hemiparesis." That's a fancy way of saying one-sided weakness. I am determined to break free of this misery.

# *New Beginning*

I stayed at Sierra Providence for seven weeks and NeuroRestorative for another seven weeks. NeuroRestorative, an inpatient therapy facility, was a different story from the hospital. COVID came and the family and friends were out. The occupational therapists, speech therapists, physical therapists, psychotherapists (the inpatient facility had a lot of "therapists"), yoga teacher, cafeteria workers, and other patients--we were a family, for good or bad. And I graduated from a wheelchair to a walker.

This was a time for reflection and calmness. I don't know what it would have been like without COVID. It was lonely, but nice, nevertheless. Before the meaning of COVID finally settled, you could go out into the backyard, or Mark and I would sneak back to the office part of the building to visit. But then COVID really bumped up. Nobody could come into NeuroRestorative.

At mealtimes, the patients had a table by themselves, a COVID addition. After we ate dinner, at about 5 o'clock and until we went to bed, we would play games, do some laundry, watch TV in our room or in the main room. Or, in my case, exploration using my walker!

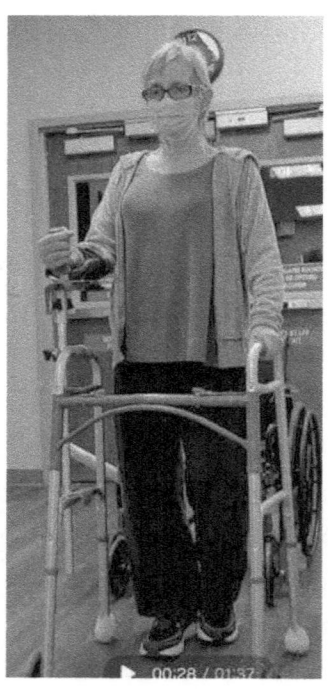

*On Walkabout with Walker*

At physical therapy, the exercises were repetitive and monotonous, but I didn't use the numbers and counts at all. Strange for a ballet instructor. I would mix them up or forget them altogether. Spelling challenges me now, and synonyms, but I did know the rudiments, like a large metal box with a lid on top, complete with a set of screws, bolts, and pamphlet of which goes where. I got tired of sheets of drawing, which I could do, and which way the letters would go in a sea of letters, which I could not do. And I strolled or rolled up to the male PT who was trying to put the sides along the base, but it was the top! I figured out what the problem was, and so, I would let my hand do the talking. It was a lot of fun.

Poker was fun! I didn't know I could do that. Handknitting or finger looping the quilt or blanket was fun, I didn't know I could do that either, and with my left hand! Team sports like cornhole and ladder toss, what a drag; I didn't like them. Besides, the walker would get in the way.

And one ballet class at NeuroRestorative, by myself, at the *barre*! It reminded me I was still me. Plié, turned out and the music was divine! Just a stretch, reclaiming strength, discipline, and joy. It gave me some hope, especially when COVID had the upper hand.

Now I do like ballet, and I do like the *corps de ballet*, the regimen, the 'heaviness,' the working as one, but I didn't like the tedium. I like to be in charge. I do like the enjoyment of movement, the pleasure of figuring out what the director wants, the diversion of music...so naturally I like to be at the helm leading the dancers or students myself. This is what I would think about at NeuroRestorative!

I miss them, the patients, and the staff. The patients – the guy that hums a little tune with flip-flop shoes, the boy who had a concussion, and the rib and spine had a rigid "cage," to offset the back turn and dip to one side. He had a skateboard accident. The Mexican woman who had a car crash with no safety belt. She had a broken or severed back and two hands that were broken too. I watched her at the PT's raised her up to an apparatus that would help her to stand on her feet. It reminded me of why I, and she, never gave up.

The staff – they were all there to keep the patients, like me, from getting depressed. We would have a schedule – wake up at 6:30 am, the nurses would bathe you, or you'd make your own slippery attempt. Blood pressure and pills by 7:00 am. Be at breakfast by 8:00 am, and we waited like school kids for the doors to be opened at 9:00 am, ready for a day of yoga, speech, exercise, gardening, cooking, drawing. Lunch at 12:00 pm and then we would start up again. It was rigid, but oddly comforting.

When I was to be discharged, Mark drove to NeuroRestorative, and I came out to him with a walker in a long procession with a big fanfare of Occupational Therapists, Physical Therapists, Speech Therapists. All were cheering and clapping, and Mark thought it was cool. Hey, maybe I was a star. No, I was embarrassed, but I was going home! That was all that mattered.

## *Coming Home*

I came home and started walking. Time to try and walk with a cane. Enough of the wheelchair and walker, I'm through with you! I think about it now; how long will I have to wait? I tried using the cane once at NeuroRestorative, but I got it all confused, my bad, and the administrator and therapist huffed away. But I was going to try. And so, I did. It was hard and, yet so easy! Whoever said it's hard and you should be afraid? I did! This was to be my woe, afraid and timid in walking, and speaking, too. I've been at this problem many times. I've worked at this, but some day it will be easier.

*Navigating the Homefront*

It was good to be home but eventually Mark and I grew restless. Very early on, it became all about how much company I needed, and, *with emphasis*, didn't. I think we got it all sorted out, but it was a learning process of being at home. Doing the laundry, making breakfast, cleaning up, exercising. I didn't drive, so Mark had to double up on the driving.

I like to get out in the world, so to speak. I felt like the hospital, NeuroRestorative, and COVID had me cooped up, and I wanted to see want the world had for me. I mean I'm still walking with a limp, my hand is curled up and my arm is listless, and my speech is horrible. But that is ok, I'm ok, at least for now.

My sons would come over, one at the time, and see how we were doing. Smith, my older son, made the best pasta, salad, and salmon dinners, and Hayden, my younger son, brought us chocolate and he or I would choose something to watch on the TV. Sounds mundane, but we enjoyed it. After all the hubbub, things have just settled down here. I can think!

Mark and I have a routine of walking, exercises, and summer swimming. Up in the suburbs, you can see the mountains, and the neighborhood has a pool. By 7 o'clock we would swim. Mark would help me do the crawl, because I have a bum right arm. I can do the back stroke. It's the nicest thing, to be out in water back stroking, and looking up at the wide West Texas sky. Nothing to do, and nowhere to be. It's lovely.

I painted, I wrote, I even gardened, all with my non-dominant hand! Anything that kept me busy, with purpose, and mobility. I went to the ballet and to UTEP Dance programs, poetry readings, prose readings, and art shows. I was even appointed as a member of the Occupational Therapist's Board at UTEP.

Lynne Grossman, a ballet friend of mine (and the real Sleeping Beauty!) helped me with ballet on Zoom. Thank God for Zoom! I re-learned all the French terms, re-learned barre movement, (just the left leg, and not very well), re-trained in modern dance. My speech was never very good, but I would try to develop some skills in my arm, hand, and fingers to try and "say" things that I couldn't say with my mouth.

And the writing and typewriting too. I had a hard time reconciling myself to the end of my career. At times I thought I could continue, using only my left hand and arm! It was impossible. I thank the chairwoman and UTEP for bringing me to my senses.

*Still Life with Roses (Left-handed Hobby!)*

Life went on.

Many friends picked me up for lunch, and that was a godsend for Mark and me. I flew on trips, including a trip to meet my sister Cookie for a stay in the wine country. I've been on girls' trips with my sisters, cousins, and friend; I even flew to San Diego solo! Traveling is good for people like me, new faces, new vistas, new challenges!

I attended the National Association for Poetry Therapy (NAPT) in Bethesda, Washington, this time with Mark, thinking that is exactly what I needed. I like NAPT very much! I recited two of my poems in the open mic poetry sessions, "Inscrutability" and "Falling." I even had the wherewithal to go up and introduce myself to Todd Boss who was standing in a TAPIT (There's a Poem in That) booth. That meeting turned into a later TAPIT interview and original poem he wrote for me. The podcast and poem can be found at: poeminthat.com.

*My Podcast Debut*

At home, I would practice the letters and parts of speech. Jackie, my speech therapist, helped me on Zoom. Mayra, the physical therapist, would help me with movement of the right leg, whether up and down the steps, or on the Pilates Reformer, or using balls, a bike, weights, dance barres, or some other equipment! I've known both women for a long time. They are in their late 30s or early 40s, and I had the pleasure of watching them go out, start a business, and work their tails off, all the while being wives and mothers. It's my pleasure to promote these two fantastic women.

- Jacqueline Alvarado, the founder of El Paso Aphasia Connection Center, a Nonprofit Organization. (915) 820-3944

- Mayra Nevarrete, the Complete Performance Physical Therapy, PLLC, 780 Resler Dr, 79912, (915) 626-5358

# In Praise of Your Aphasia

## *For Lisa*

What a beautiful dance you

              dance here for us,

                            who sit in our

darkness,

        programs in our laps.

                      What a raw, sensuous

    tension you sustain

           along the body's limber

borders. How well you

        remind us: any dance

                worth doing is

struggle.

        There must be a word

                  (French, feminine?) for

the mirror

    behind the barre of the mind

                beyond which

no stroke survivor sees. Seize, survivor, stroke – no, seize

again -- & we

              seize with you to survivor her, too.

                       We

see her. We

            watch you wake &

                             wick her.

                                                        All dance is séance,

flames a-flicker. You swirl
                    & swivel, unhinged. It's

                                                        haunting.

    On toe-tips,

        fingertips, tip of

                    tongue,

                                                        it's ghosts

whose unsung song you
conjure,


                    flaunting physical laws.

                                                        Do you

        hear our one-

                    handed applause?




                                                        Todd Boss

## *Falling*

I fell today.
I've been falling,
falling the past three years. Inside six times,
outside in the yard two times,
going someplace two times (that
was embarrassing!).

I've been falling
over words, too. Countless
adverbs, spelling, pronouncing
and numbers.

But I go on, right or wrong, like
some dumb animal.
How does the song go?
"I picked myself up, brushed myself off, and
started all over again."
Again, and again.

## *Inscrutability*

Enigma, isolation, inscrutability,
that is what my brain, my mind, is like. That is
supposed to be what we say about the
Chinese, Japanese, Vietnamese,
but the cranes, the art, the tea leaves, they
are strange, beautiful, exciting. Could it be
that my brain/mind,
all the synapses, neurons, axons,
will be strange and beautiful and exciting?


Look up, the flock of birds flew into the sky, scatted,
in disarray, the way my mind is.

Chinese Magpie birds are named for "happiness."

# *Mark's Interview*

*How did you feel about the onset of the stroke, and particularly when Dr. Payne said that I wouldn't talk or walk anymore?*

I was pretty much in shock and disbelief, and I just discounted the possibility that that was going to be the case. I was confident that you were going to be OK, or at least I refused to believe anything different.

*I noticed the way you correct yourself. Like "my car" to "our cars," or "I want" to "we want." I like that.*

Well, me too. Everything we share. Everything.

*How do you feel when I can't find the word or phrase I'm looking for? Is it confusing?*

Well, it's frustrating and it's confusing of course because I'm not getting the right word you're looking for. But I'm sure it's much more frustrating for you than it is for me, so I just shut up and wait.

*When I get mad because of the stroke, does that make you feel helpless?*

I feel unhappy because you're in a place that I don't want you to be, but I understand that sometimes these things happen and hopefully it will pass. So, I don't feel helpless, I just wait it out.

*How are you caring for our animals?*

I enjoy taking care of the pets. I think they really improve our lives. We appreciate their company. They entertain us, they love us. I, very happily, take care of the animals because I think they make our house a better place.

*How much additional work do you have to do because of my stroke?*

You mean the lawn, cleaning up the porch and patio, all that stuff? Yeah, and then I have to go back to work. But I have a great sense of purpose which makes it all pretty easy to take.

*How is your life?*

Checking in on my life, you mean? My life with you? Well, it's changed in that I really don't want to be out of the house more than necessary. I want to be available to you. I plan my day in that fashion, so, I'm not going to be gone longer than necessary. I try to keep tabs on the chores, so they don't stack up and you're not frustrated with, you know, the house being disorganized or stuff like that? I happily do these things because I love you so much and I want us to have a good life here. I know it's very frustrating for you because these are things you would prefer to do yourself, and I appreciate that, and I don't feel burdened because I know you would be doing these things yourself if you could.

# *Teaching a Class*

"Athletes, dancers, and musicians are driven to get better." -- Peter Levine

I wanted to teach the Aphasia and Brain Injury group a lesson in dance. Dance is beautiful and mathematically precise. Big bold bodies moving through the air, smiling or being concentrated. The exercise regimen Gyrokinesis is like that, a movement so exact and rigorous, and you can do it seated! One friend, Denise Tokopf, had been trained in it, and I wanted to train myself. She would come over and get me once a month, drive me to her house for training, have a good lunch (she would make lunch!), and then drive me home. Nice!

I was so darn nervous in the classroom! At home, I would practice, not the movement, but the letters and parts of speech. Jackie helped me, and every Friday from April till June, we sat there on ZOOM, and, together, we would hash out words for the dance and exercising. Jackie joked she didn't know all the parts of the dance, but she knew it by now! My friends, Ana for Tap and Jennifer for Breath Work, would help me with the dancing, and I would do the Gyrokinesis and Modern Dance. I called it "Empowered Steps, Dancing with Aphasia and Brain

Injuries," and the Theater and Dance Department at UTEP were kind enough to let us hold the class in the studio.

The first year, everybody was there, Aphasia and brain injuries and their caregivers. I invited the Occupational Therapist, and the Yoga teacher, from NeuroRestorative, and the Physical Therapist from Sierra Providence, whom I had taught at UTEP! KVIA, the TV station, was there in the last class of the eight parts of the session.

The second year, we had a performance by Zuill Bailey, a cellist. He played Bach's Cello Suite No. 1 in G Major, Prelude. Aphasia and brain injury danced to the recording of Zuill playing his cello, tap, poetry, and each person saying and performing their own dance adjectives, like love, relaxing, handsome, and crazy.

"Gyrokinesis" is a practice that coordinates movement, breath and mental focus. Using the rhythmic pattern and flowing sequences, it can be adapted to anyone's ability, and it may be seated as well. That's crucial! I could have used seated Yoga or exercise posture, but I wanted the twisting and turning. The sequencing, "Proud Peacock," "Sitz Bones," "Barber Pole," "Paddling," and "Locked In," stroke and brain injuries need that, and besides a dancer, Hungarian born Juliu Horvath, had invented Gyrokinesis or Gyrotonic. (The Gyrokinesis Exercises will be covered in subsequent chapters.)

## DANCING WITH APHASIA AND BRAIN INJURY

**THURSDAY JUNE 13 - JULY 25**
**5 - 6 PM; FOX FINE ARTS BUILDING, M201**

Our class will be seated Gyrokinesis exercise, tap and modern dance. Wheelchairs are welcome!

Independence Day, Thursday – University Closed

 915-820-3944
jacqueline.epaphasia@gmail.com

## *The Art of Falling*

Yes, it is! Elizabeth Bishop, an American poet and Pulitzer Prize winner, the author of "One Art," had a sardonic saying that "the art of losing isn't very hard to master." The art of falling was pretty hard to master. Everything, falling too, is frustrating, maddeningly daunting. Contrary to my poems, I fell in the backyard and the house a number of times. Now when I go anywhere, I use "caution sense." I feel exasperated and defeated. When one ought to feel *I-got-it-now*, caution reigns over me. I mean, I am a dancer! Used to be, before my stroke, I was free, confident, but now I've been taught that the world is a scary place.

And now the speech. In the hospital, Mark said when he asked what I thought of Medicare, and I responded, clear as a bell, "community theatre." It is a mystery how the brain works. I am Expressive aphasia, or Broca. The Mayo Clinic explains that:

- Expressive aphasia (sometimes called Broca's or nonfluent aphasia) in which people are better at understanding others than they are at speaking. They often struggle to get words out or to speak in phrases, rather than complete sentences.

- Comprehensive aphasia (sometimes called fluent or Wernicke's aphasia) in which people tend to speak in long, complex sentences that don't make sense. They may have difficulty understanding spoken language, and do not always realize that others can't understand them.

- Global aphasia. People with that pattern tend to have poor comprehension and difficulty forming words and sentences.

You know, I didn't reach any closure or a-ha, like the stroke authors or any nonfiction memoirs claim to have done. I really didn't. But I think about it now. How was my life? Was kind of life would I believe in? I will never be a tenured professor, never again be a dance instructor, but who do I want to be? Essays, short stories, and poems were my genres, as ballet and modern dance had been before. Well, ever since the stroke, I did the poetry and modern dance. What now?

*Elizabeth Bishop's poem:*

# One Art

The art of losing isn't hard to master:
so many things seem filled with intent
to be lost that their loss is no disaster.

Lose something every day. Accept the fluster
of lost door keys, the hour badly spent.
The art of losing isn't hard to master.

Then practice losing farther, losing faster: places,
and names, and where it was you meant to travel.
None of these will bring disaster.

I lost my mother's watch. And look! my last, or
next-to-last, of three loved houses went.
The art of losing isn't hard to master.

I lost two cities, lovely ones. And vaster, some
realms I owned, two rivers, a continent. I miss
them, but it wasn't a disaster.

--Even losing you (the joking voice, a gesture
I love) I shan't have lied. It's evident

the art of losing's not too hard to master
though it may look like (*Write* it) like disaster.

*My poem:*
*Elizabeth Bishop- "the art if losing isn't very hard to master."*

# Two Art or Aphasia

If the art of losing isn't very hard to master,
Then I'm frustrated, it
is clear that Bishop
grants intent. No big
moment, it is her
loss, no disaster.

But I've lost something else. Accept the fluster
for the loss of the
right leg, arm, and my
brain is spent! No, the
art of losing isn't
hard to master.

Then I've got to practice my walking, losing footing faster
than I've ever had to pick my brain,
 and lift my arm with hell-bent
progress. That is no lie! Ah, the ruin of
me, that disaster!

My loss is the
uprooting of my care,
or watch, my last, or

next-to-last, of two loved
limbs and a brain in descent.
The art of losing, really, isn't hard to master.


I lost two limbs, lovely ones. And, vaster,
some rites I disowned, but one appendage,
 my insistent mind. I miss them, but it
wasn't a disaster.

--Even losing me, my one voice,
a gesture I love, that is a problem.
It's evident
the art of losing's not too hard to master
though it may look like
(*Write* it with the left hand!) like disaster.

# *The Power of Forgetting*

I'm lost! The power of forgetting is massive! I can understand if I'm old or had a stroke, both of which are true. But I know myself, and forgetting it is something that I don't do. I forgot the names of political candidates or celebrities. Last time, when talking to Mark about the TV movies, I said, "Zack Bacharach" when I know I should have said "Ben Stiller!" Or Facebook and TikTok - rabbit holes, I know they are counting on the power of forgetting! Or questioning, did I take the pill or am I forgetting the time?

No, I'm talking about everyday things like trash cans, mascara, cereal, and toothpaste. It's exhausting! I can't pronounce them, or I just erase them from my brain. For instance, I promised myself that I would exercise, which is a "must do" thing when you have a stroke. I put it down in my notebook, and I forgot. Flash, and it was gone.

But then when I have to concentrate, really concentrate, I'm desolate or detached or numb. I cannot think. In writing this book I am terribly slow. Slow concept, large and little ones. Big concept, I want to write a chapter or two, or a little one, like how do you spell "concept"?

I'm trying to stay on top of this thing, this massive, and problem-filled thing. I'm writing poetry and memoirs just because I know there is knowledge in my brain that I can no longer express at the time they come to me. In other words, I know where my brain isn't liable to go!

## *Words Like Water*

*I am going to try that*, I thought, *words like water.* I was stuck with my non-word, and then I panicked. *Oh, no,* I thought, *my brain is locked up; come on, brain! I don't know what to do now. Help!* I wanted to express myself! All the other people with Aphasia and brain injury wanted to express themselves, too.

In April 2025, I went to the National Association of Poetry Therapy in Portland, Oregon, and I kept hearing about the words and lines of poetry. I thought of my manuscript, my book that was on my computer. How many words and lines of poetry are there in my book? Lots of them, 15,350 words before the book editor cleaned it up.

I feel so grown up! Not a baby anymore. I like it; it's important to be in control and *fast*, at least it is for me. And not so fast that I lose my composure, but fast, nevertheless. I dance fast, I choreograph fast, I write fast, and I move through people fast, that is the downfall of me. But not of my students and not of my family. (Do I?)

I am comfortable without "talking" when I can express myself through dance. Whether it's comics or highbrow, choreographer or dance performer, I am easy with that. But you know what is up ahead. It's all *choreographed!* Same with poetry and short stories, a novel, and essay. You are the author, a poet, a mastermind. Arrange the words, the letters *in* the words, who is speaking and who is not speaking. But now I am nothing, a void. I think of the words so eloquent, so fine. Whatever is below the surface, hidden in the cobwebs is that unknowable word, or a number!

In Switzerland, I could not be me without the word, it was all like yes (ja) and no (nein), and by the third year I could say, "Guten tag, kannst du mir einen Gefallen tun?" But I had a book (das Buch) and lots of theatre friends (die bühne Freunde).

El Paso is a border city; it's right on the Rio Grande. Aphasia is like living on the border, and I want to cross over but for the fog. I can't seem to get around the haze, but I forgot about the water! My fog, it's made up of water. Water flowing down, and around, seeping through my mind, like a deep open crack, dripping along to a brain valley. Words like water!

*Comic* Me and Michelle

# *High Brow*

*Kendall Cherry Beasley, Choreographer*

*Choreographed*   Lucia Uhl, *photographer*

## *Oh, The Pearls!*

I woke up and it was cold. Where were my socks? I investigated the dresser drawer and found some, and found something else, too. It was a satin jewelry organizer bag that was supposed to have the pearls inside. But there were no pearls! They were gone!

Oh, the pearls! I had a nice warm feeling of places I would go with the pearls. Late at night, I would go to the ballet or opera. In the afternoon I'd go for tea with a girlfriend. Not really, but I could if I wanted to. I could hold on to that dream, that anticipation, that nostalgia. I tore through my stuff, my clothes, everything! I took it all out and put it back.

I corrupted my channel of frantic thought and stroke-induced craziness. Maybe the boys, Hayden or Smith, could have taken the pearls, or maybe it was one of their friends they brought to the garage to hear their music and talk politics into the wee hours of the night.

I talked to Hayden. "Mom, I'm sure no one stole your pearls. Besides, the dogs would let you know." That's right! The dogs, three of them, would bark.

I thought, *the maid*. She could have taken the pearls. And then I got blue. The maid would NOT have taken the pearls, Lisa. How could you even think that? And how could you think of the boys? *Because I'm desperate!*

I settled down. Then I forgot. Typical.

Well, I've found not my pearls, but the picture of my pearls. The picture was right up behind the passports in my dresser drawer. They were not in the satin necklace organizer bag. The pearls were in a box with a blue swede cover with two snaps and a white satin interior. I took this picture many years ago because if we were ever robbed, I wanted proof for the insurance company. I didn't know that I would be the one to investigate!

Now tell me, old person or stroke survivor?

*Okay, it's probably all of the above. . .a crazy old stroke survivor!*

# *Grief*

Half of One, Half of Another One

5 Steps of Grief – Denial, Anger, Bargaining, Depression, Acceptance – *Kubler-Ross*

Denial helps me move a little closer…to what? I don't know, independence? That was a good thing, right? I worked at it, so did a lot of stroke victims/survivors. To me, "independent" would mean I am being brave, not a co-dependent, being me! Not too independent! But rather semi-independent. I don't want to be an "indifferent" person.

Anger? Depression? I go back and forth, finding a new way to live. And bargaining; well, I don't know. Bargaining is a slippery slope!

"I will gladly pay you Tuesday for a functioning right arm today." Probably not.

\*\*\*

Anger/Acceptance: I lost my tenure at UTEP. It was cold and daunting. I was at home, and I thought I was going for a pep talk with my chairperson. You know, how it was going to be, how it was NOT going to be. Mark got me ready for the

Zoom call. He said, "Are you good?" "No problem," I said, "I got this," and he slipped out. I thought, *now let me see if I can figure out how this Zoom thing works,* and up popped the chairwoman and another new person, a female lawyer with short, bobbed hair, short-cropped bangs and horn-rimmed glasses. She wore a suit and "comfortable" black shoes and had a file in her hands. What was the chairwoman doing to me?

Because we were collegial friends, I didn't think she would pull that one. She was nervous, cold. But I was nervous, too.

At that point my screen went dark, and I was trying to make sense of things, but as usual my brain didn't help. Mark was there, but remember when I said, "Not too independent?" I needed Mark at that moment. It was brutal. I went over, and over, and over that moment again before I realized I could do something else, something more challenging and more worthwhile. I decided I was going to teach movement and dance for people with aphasia and brain injury. (The chairwoman was gone by the next semester!)

Depression/Acceptance: I did get depressed, but then I got better. It's the yin yang. Isn't that the way for most people? As a stroke survivor, you have days of frustration and exasperation. It hardly even matters if you just pulled yourself up out of the mud. You still must get with the program. "But wait a minute, I'm just trying to keep up!" Or you can sit in the dark and say, "I'm no good. Yes, I've tried, but it was a waste."

Now I am a free bird. I didn't get closure or anything like that. I just kind of stopped. No closure, no fanfare, no acceptance of the life I would be living. But life showed me there was a different path, a new something, something big and important.

I've read and heard some incredible stories about people who have survived in the face of insurmountable odds. There was a stroke survivor who had "locked-in syndrome," and couldn't move below her neck. She had to use a speech board to "talk" with her eyes. Or the man with ALS who also had to "talk" with his eyes. Or the teacher who had rapidly advancing pneumonia, which was both viral and bacterial, and had to have her hands and legs amputated. On the TV, there were little children with cancer or bone deformities.

I stopped looking. Everyone has something or at least has someone who has got something.

According to the American Stroke Association, each year in the United States there are 795,000 strokes, and 610,000 of these are first-time strokes. 610,000! How many American can there be?

340.1 million apparently. Mark tells me that is 0.18% of the population (did I mention he is an accountant?). And how many are afflicted with amputations, Parkinson's, cerebral palsy, or the children who are born with cleft palates, or conjoined twins?

Virginia Woolf, the British writer, said, "There is a kind of sadness that comes from knowing too much, for seeing the world as it truly is. It is the sadness of understanding that life is not a grand adventure, but a series of small, insignificant moments ...and in that understanding, there is a profound loneliness, a sense of being cut off from the world, from other people, from oneself." I think she was writing about love, but isn't that also true about illness or loss?

I have made a new life for myself, writing poetry and teaching those with stroke and brain injury. I'm writing all the time. It's important to find something that you absolutely love doing, then stick with it!

# *Gyrokinetic Exercise*

1. Proud peacock and Bow Shape.

    a. Move head and chest like a proud peacock (the head will be up & back). The arms are loose, and the shoulders are back. The legs and feet are turned outward. The lumbar spine needs to move forward and up.

    b. Curl your head down to make a bow shape with the eyes on the belly. Your arms and shoulders will be turned inward. The legs and feet are turned inward. The spine needs to move down and the letter "C.

2. Imagine there is glass in front of you and behind. Don't press the glass!

    a. Bend over to the Right and up. Bend over to the Left. Go farther!

    b. Take the Left hand up and over, palm up, and stretch to the Right, and up. Now take the Right hand and stretch to the Left.

3. The sitz bones are the two bones in the bottom of the hips. Imagine two donuts on the seat below you.

    a. Go around the sitz bones to make a circle to the Right

with your spine. Come back to the center with your spine.

    b. Go around the sitz bones to make a circle to the Left and come back to the center with your spine. A circle and a circle make figure 8.

    c. Three directives. Rib, shoulder, and head (like a pencil drawing on the ceiling).

4. A barber pole

    a. Spiral the spine to the Right. Imagine someone has called you from the back. Take the Left hand and push on the Left knee and spiral around the spine to the Right and come back.

    b. Place your Right hand on your Right knee and spiral around to the Left and come back.

5. Paddling.

    a. Reach up like "in the morning", head looking up.

    b. Cup your hand Right around the base of the skull. Put BOTH hands around the base of head.

    c. Turn to the Right, bend over, move your Left elbow down and Right elbow up.

    d. Sitting upright, turn to the Left, move the Right elbow up and the Left elbow down.

    e. Go forward and back.

6. Lock together.

   a. Put your feet together or at least 1 inch apart.

   b. Put your Right hand on the Left side and thrust it down. The Right forearm and Left knee will 'lock' together. The spine's down and to the right.

      c. The Right ribs will be touching the Right thigh.

   d. The Left hand will drop down, bring it up extended to the wall in front of you, then up and back. Your eyes and face will follow.

   e. Pull around the chest. The spine needs to be up erect.

   f. Put your Left hand on the Right side and thrust it down. Your Left forearm and Right knee will "lock" together. The spine's down and to the left.

   g. The Right hand will drop down, to the mirror, and up and back. The eyes and face will follow.

*Class Demonstration*

# Poetry

# *When I Was a Tiny One or The Stroke Survivor*

When I was a tiny one I
lived in a vast sea,
>   tossed by the wave, back
>   and forth, ingrained with
>   sand and poetry.

Or maybe I lived in the wood forest.
>   It was cold there,
>   snow twirls, lies dormant,
>   twirls some more.
>   I did that too.

Or maybe I lived in a hospital.
>   Up all night,
>   cheery doctor and nurses,
>   feet shuffle, open door.
>   Surprise!

I can't speak. Surprise!
I can't move my arm. Cheers!
I have a wheelchair. Bottoms up!


But I was older then. A stroke Took
me by surprise!

## *A Brand New World Opens Before Me*

Strange, I woke up to find that I really didn't want to wake up. I was stunned, mesmerized, dumb.
A stroke had erased all the good and bad, and I saw a brand new world opens before me.

I saw the right side of my body, arm and leg, was new. I had to learn how to speak, how to spell, was new.
I, slowly, re-trained how to be dependent, humble, quiet. A brand new world opens before me.

New husband, new boys – they are men now, new me, new faces, old faces, faces of my friends I never see, faces I saw, really saw, or the landscaping, or the clouds.

A brand new world opens before me.

## *Numb*

Numbness, speechlessness.
Why does my speech not reach out? Why
does my brain not reach out? Why does
my soul not reach out?
Used to be, before the stroke, I had a hole in my head, a vestal,
a
    divine presence.

Used to be consumed with my ballet and poetry, they come
running down,
    down, down.
It all stopped-


My body needs to dance or do some choreography.
My speech needs to say things, talk about ideas, expressive like
love, or
    politics, or migrant farm workers, or mundane things like
    "vacuuming the house."

The numb lessness, the speechlessness, the
brainlessness,
the soullessness,
I want to be a Helper, a Choreographer, a Star, or a
savvy home builder,
or a crime buster, or

a microbiologist,
not the old, crippled, stay in the home wife. I won't!

## *Two Birds and One Aphasia*

We were talking, he and I, about
two birds,
one a Sparrow, one a Woodpecker, with
a feeder on the branch outside.

With my arm up and hand in a fist, I
said "crouder,"
he said "crowder?" I
said "clourage," he
said "cloud?"
I said "cruder,"
He said "prouder?" And
so on, and so on.

Two birds had flown away.

## *What Are You Reading Right Now*

Don't know.
I am reading the box of cereal,
the headlines from the newspapers.
I am reading the book, though not the inside of the book.
I am prepared for the book, arranging
the book,
the clothes, the stuff
from A to Z and then I
have forgotten.

## *Falling*

I fell today.
I've been falling,
falling the past three years.
Inside six times,
outside in the yard two times,
going someplace two times (that
was embarrassing!).

I've been falling
over words, too. Countless
adverbs, spelling, pronouncing
and numbers.

But I go on, right or wrong, like
some dumb animal.
How does the song go?
"I picked myself up, brushed myself off, and
started all over again."
Again, and again.

## *Oubaitori*

I like the Japanese idea that people, "like flowers, bloom in their own time, Each one in their individual ways." Oubaitori

## *Boredom*

Antsy! What can I do? Paint, write, exercise, go outside, come inside, change all the pillows, read Facebook, go to sleep, wake up?

I'm bored.

Glass of wine? That's the ticket! And Monopoly for one. No, Checkers for one. Chess, Backgammon? I prefer Checkers. Down to earth, Checkers is. No, no, a glass of wine? I prefer Backgammon and wine. No, Chess! You know, where in the park they have those Chess players? You know, old face, old hand, black or white old men. Wait a minute, no women and no glass of wine...

I remember my mother and three other mothers, other women, playing Bridge. John Gary would sing "Yellow Bird" on the stereo. Cigarettes and Bloody Mary's and Bridge on the game table.

## *Two in Thirds*

See the difference between he and me?
Since the stroke, I've been dependent,
conscious, mute, mild.
He is independent. I want that.
I am slow because of my leg. He
is fast.
I want that.
To be free, to not be telling myself watch
out, steady, be careful!
He has flawless speech. I
want that.
I have to think about it, cutting it off in
the mid-word or mid-sentence.
See how it will be? Between he and me.

## *Inscrutability*

Enigma, isolation, inscrutability,
that is what my brain, my mind, is like. That is
supposed to be what we say about the Chinese,
Japanese, Vietnamese,
but the cranes, the art, the tea leaves, they
are strange, beautiful, exciting. Could it be
that my brain/mind,
all the synapses, neurons, axons,
will be strange and beautiful and exciting?


Look up, the flock of birds flew into the sky, scatted, in disarray, the way my mind is.

Chinese Magpie birds are named for "happiness."

## *Oh, Silent Night*

There, a silent pause, a
silent slightest mimic of
a cat paw against the
floor,
or the tick tock
of grandfather's clock, or
a heartbeat-

## *It's Christmas Time*

Hark! It's Christmas time again.
There will be snow on the mountaintop, caroling
down to our house,
our yard will be lights, a tree, and mistletoe.

Lo, it is myrrh and frankincense raining
down, running through
the arroyo, the creek bed, the river, to
the sea miles and miles away.

Angels sing, brighten the standing moon, glad
over the field of cotton and snow.
We will bring bread, fish, and wine all around. Sigh,
or not.

## *Fireworks Inside of Me*

There will be fireworks inside of me.
Great volume of sound,
great volume of words.
Stand on your feet like the roots going
downward into the earth, flowering up
and up again to the sky. Be demanding.
Be hot tempered.
There will be fireworks and bells ringing.


I don't want to be like I am.
Christmas is here,
fireworks and bells and Christmas, I
wish I may, I wish I might,
have the wish I wish tonight-


A mighty sword cut through
the bramble of my throat, the
jungle of my mind.

*Elizabeth Bishop- "the art if losing isn't very hard to master."*

## *Two Art or a Stroke*

If the art of losing isn't hard to master,
then I'm frustrated, it is clear that Bishop grants intent. No big
moment, it is her loss, no disaster.

But I've lost something else. Accept the fluster
for the loss of the right leg, arm, and my brain is spent! No, the
art of losing isn't hard to master.

Then I've got to practice my walking, losing footing faster
that I've ever had to pick my brain, and lift my arm with hell-
bent
progress. That is no lie! Ah, the ruin of me, that disaster!

My loss is the uprooting of my care, or watch, my last, or next-
to-last, of two limbs and a brain in descent.
The art of losing, really, isn't hard to master.


I lost two limbs, lovely ones. And, vaster,
some rites I disowned, but one appendage, my insistent mind.
I
miss them, but it wasn't a disaster.

--Even losing me, my one voice, a gesture I

love, that is a problem. It's evident
the art of losing's not too hard to master
though it may look like (*Write* it with the left hand!) like disaster.

## *I'm Weepy Now*

My father taught me how not to cry, not
to show any emotion.
Well, that is right and wrong.
Stoics, impartial, thinking, that is
what I used to be,
or thought to be. But
I'm weepy now.

Two faces of me, two approaches. After
the stroke I'm different,
now I am weepy at the commercials,


I cry at families,
lately at "Moonlight," or
Joni Mitchell and the Grammys.
Yes, I am weepy, now and forever more.


Lost love, about to be born love, tiny
love, big grand love.
I'm weepy now.

## *Our Dog and I, We Are a Pair!*

His name is Jack. He's got soulful eyes, intellectual,
actually, I think so.
Jack has his hind legs and hips are not good. Me?
I've got a leg and arm, both of which are not so
good, in fact they are pretty bad. Jack walks on
four legs, two that work,
I walk on two, one works, we
are a pair!

In the yard I fell, but Jack keeps muddling through. His
hind legs are deformed and crazy-like,
he is hard of hearing and can't see very well. I'm
learning to speak, but I can't speak for him. Poor
Jack, and poor me too.

I am learning from him.
For instance, he walks into the bedroom
eyeing the bed, he walks around and around and up toward the
bed, he
jumps... but he doesn't make it,
so, he goes off nonchalantly. Later on
he walked into the bedroom and, sure enough, he
hopped on the bed! Got to hand it to Jack. Me? I'm
ready for the challenge, up for the fight,
no little thing gets by me! I try one way or the other. Self-
care mantra. It's exhausting!

*"We shall overcome because the arc of the moral universe is long, but it*
*bends toward justice."*
*-Martian Luther King*

# *Justice*

Justice,
Martian Luther King used to say that
"the arc the moral universe is long but it bends towards justice."
In Justice there will be no blind, no deaf, no
crippled, no lonely.
No aphasia either, and I am one of them, Justice,
We see the blind, the deaf,
but how do we talk? And talk better!
We see the see the cripple, and I am one on them. We see farther and wider,
Justice,
We see the lonely,
I am lonely inside of myself, the
layers and layers
of myself.
Oh, I want to get out but patience calls! Brick by
brick,
I slowly made myself a new person, Not
great, but a person,

Justice,
Like the blind and deaf,
the lonely ones, the crippled, and Parkinsonians,
the autistic, the brain injured. Not great, but a
person.
Justice.

## *Oh, Melinda*

Oh, Melinda! Did you go to sleep, while the next morning, you would do some routine. Brush your teeth,
get dressed, go outside and fight the traffic to the office, or would
you tell dead Joel *I'm coming!*
Would you wake up in the middle of the night forlorn, or would
you be so sleepy that, may comfort leave,
letting go at the right moment.

## *Theft*

The crime of theft is deceiving.
It can be stealing, larceny, burglary,
ripped-off!
I was robbed – of my speech, of my writing, of
my dignity.
And the right side of my body,
the extremities were flaccid and dead cold. How
can it be that my arm was snatched up? My leg was
a fraud,
how can it be?
The breaking and entering of my brain? A
mugging!
It's amazing to me now, the heist was sneaky,
while I was asleep, the shoplifting ghosts came and got the loot!

## *Beautiful Toes*

I'm beautiful right down to my toes!
Well, one toes, the other toes
were grotesque!
I detest those toes!


And leg, one of my beautiful legs!


I was watching tennis,
Djokovic vs Alcaraz,
pretty men, graceful, athletic.
They ran right up to the net,
turned around and ran back.


What was that run like?

# *A Baby's Wonder*

The people are so savvy,
they know so much, politics, science, history. I'm a
baby, after the stroke, I see the world with infant
eyes.
I fall all the time; I speak with a baby tongue. The
world is new to me,
a baby's wonder.


My family teaches me how to use words in order.
My speech therapist teaches me how to make sense of syntax.
My
physical therapist teaches me how to walk.

I cry at certain times, but then I'm happy again, a
baby curiosity, amazement, bewilderment.
I stay behind the adult and nod, brow furled, but
I'm just a little newborn.

## *A Song*

Let me hear a song with the bee and flower, lift up
the world in this moment, in this hour.
Would luck be an answer, like a four-leaf clover or the
show and power and the shiny glow, or like the sun?
Give it up for the peaches and plums,
let the ant, beetles, snails have their moments, and
the birds with their feathers up in a whirl. Can you
believe it? For a light-filled eyeblink, a heartbeat,
the world and sun twirl
away.

## *Misunderstanding*

I can't stand it. I speak and
no one knows
what the hell I'm trying to say, well,
some people, but nobody. not my
husband,
not the speech therapist, not
the friends,
not the enemies,
not the whole bloody continent!

I wonder if I spoke Spanish, or
French,
or German,
or even Arabic.
How do you say, in Arabic, "I'm
listening, I'm fascinated, tell all,
please!"

I can't help the puddle I get into, I
struggled,
I cajoled,
I smiled the big smile,
it's a problem.
I say "yes" or "no".

# *A New Beginning*

A new beginning, a new chapter, but
I don't know how I am supposed to do it. My
loss of something old, and brittle?
My speech, arm, and leg? No,
it's bigger than that, something new, something
'you.'
As soon as you look down in the shallow bit of
the river, you found a pebble, a stone.
When you throw, or part, with the piece of rock, It
will skip, dart, and hurtle
In the freshwater, that will be me.

## *And So, We Shall Rise, Fall and Rise*

Winter, the storm bristles and we die, we all do, a
stroke is like that.

In Spring, we grow plumlike, and all is sunny and bright, trees
blossom, leaves grow, fruits firm and juicy,

There is the Summer, plum and peaches sigh and weight of
breaths.

But Fall is to ward the cold, the leaves blow to ground, A
deer, two deer now, a foal and his mother.

A season. Rise and fall, like bread, fold on fold, We say,
"I knew her," or "I knew him,"

And so, we shall rise, fall and rise.
Like the swallows, I rise. My name is Risen,

## *Hear! Hear! The Caregivers!*

Hear! Hear! The caregivers! The
stalwart, the share givers!

Benevolent and considerate, oh,
let us say passionate!

I can think of some folks
who are kind and noble.

We who are in the abyss, the
black hole, try to miss

each joy, each merit of love and
lost, must play the part of

Winners. Handshakes and applause, smile
and be grateful,
stroke, brain injuries, yes, even paralyzed, be
saintly and graceful.

Superman died in a flurry of flashbulbs, press
coverage, documentaries on the TV. Superman's
wife died, afterward, of cancer, with her children
and nothing left to release.

# 1998 Poems

# *Vintage*

She spoke of the soul in her wine.
How she loved to cook while sipping a good red. Inhaling
the scent of onion, garlic, oil,
she would sip the smoke and fire in her glass, drink
it down into to her belly.

Where Spanish heels crack against the floor,
and gypsies wail of lost love in the mountain caves.


Where a low moon rises red over Bedouins
camped in the African desert.

Where a finger smeared with crimson earth reaches
up to paint of the hunt.

All this she found in her glass,
a spell conjured up from the heart and the grape.


I grabbed my glass of wine and drank deeply, held my
breath while the warmth ran through me, lifted my eyes
to the wine,
and met the reflection of my blank, expectant face.

# *My Children and the Sea*

I. Older Son

A collection of jumbled limbs thrown against the bed, hurtled
through wind and fury to this abrupt, temporary stop. Tangled
hair flung wide over pillow, brow and beyond,
hands webbed with rumpled bedding.
He sleeps in the shipwreck of gnarled seaweed sheets
while electricity crackles in the clouds above.
I bend in the eye of the storm to check his breath
 so soft I have to strain to hear it.


II. Younger Son

The light frames his smallness as he sleeps.
Round and pale, a moonlit beach pebble.
His hand presses against the wall,
a chubby starfish clinging to the side of a ship.
Small passenger in a rough sea,
he hangs there tightly, as if his grasp
could stay the frantic pace, calm the raging surf.

III We Three

Smooth and slippery, we are swimming,
arcing over, under, around each other.
Fins for feet we navigate our journey

following stars, the news, a hunch.
I teach them tricks, feed them treats,
stroke their silky dolphin backs,
and ease their captivity until
I turn them out to sea.

# *5BDR, 4BA + MAID'S*

There they sit, Los Comandantes, solid,
massive, intractable.
A residential Mount Rushmore.
Spread out across the hill,
they simmer
in the shimmering heat
daring us to pass between their burly shoulders butted up
against each other.

Like a fist slammed down on a table,
they are planted squarely on spaces both
illogical and ill-fitting,
spit-polished and defiant. Windows
stare, unblinking.
With the earth crumbling under their weight
they cast down dry rock and dead branches,
scraps for the unwashed.

Clearly, they are saying something
important about arrival, conquest,
who's who in the 'hood?
Looking up toward this ersatz Olympus, we
scratch our head and wonder
what language are they speaking?

## *Hard and Bitter as a Rusted Nail*

Hard and bitter as a rusted nail,
she scratched her name across the page and
wondered when, exactly,
had she come to this place. Where
had she crossed the last remaining
line that left her here at the edge of
all decency,
caused her to plunge head-long and flailing with
one swift slash of her hand
across a pile of paper.
Her signature didn't even look like her handwriting. She
was already fading from the picture,
being replaced by something foreign. Something
that could do what she had done. Someone who
could turn away.
Someone who could look into the face of a
child's raw pleading
and turn away.

# *The World is so Beautiful, I Must be Dying*

Walk softly, lest we crack that perfect blue glass sky,
cloud-licked and looming. Who knows what
terrible perfection lies nimbus-tethered, spinning
silver lining within.

Today the wind races through the pines down
to a desert spitting bloom,
laying waste to the cynic, sending
cats mad with sunshine to swat
ghosts in my window.

And did you see that man? The one who gave
his woman an eighteen-year grin?
And young sons warm in their beds, cherry
cheeks ripe to their mother's kisses.

I see it all, under the blue glass sky,
nestled up against the mountainside.
I see it now, briefly, like pink blossoming
pear trees, hooting like the wind down to the
desert floor under the beds of
ripe cheeked boys. Oh, walk softly, I
must be dying.

# *Mercy*

*For Ela*

Time leans on a stick, hobbling forward
into your room, your bed where hands,
like aged roots, fold, unfold, then lie still
under tired veins pulsing faintly, a
mapping memory,
>   pulling fish from the Brazos,
>   stuffing silken parachutes into neat WWII packages,
>   serving
>   barbeque and Pabst on the porch, Hud's doves
>>   quiet in their coop over your
>>   riotous red gladioli.

Again, your hands wave good-bye to one brother off to drive cattle.
Again, your hand plants another brother young and legless into
>   the ground.

Again, you are reaching for sweet Hud in his breathless night.


The last time we visited the home we brought a hyacinth, blue like your mapping veins. You wore your teeth for us. We didn't come again, felt your hands let us go.

## *Legacy*

My arms draw S's in the blue-green water,
My legs open and close like
    long white scissor blades under the surface.
I flirt with local boys, a red-haired farm boy
    who had lost an arm in a tractor accident,
His cousin, a dark-haired boy with silver-capped teeth, says he
    rides rodeo in De Soto.
I flirt with those boys, in pink,
    a new bikini. I am young, almost beautiful,
    I think.
Across the pool, my grandmother sits
    at the water's edge. Her thick legs planted
squarely on wet pavement, her skirt rising
in the breeze, revealing
    her slip and stocking rolled around elastic
    garters at her knee.
My grandmother's wispy hair, reddish-
brown and dyed, flies undirected, crazy
about her face. She squints through
glasses, a tarnished chain
    looping down around slumping small
    town shoulders.

What is she to me, I think?
To my long legs? To my pink bikini flush in the sudden chill
of
    summer's water?

# *I Dreamed We Were Young*

I dreamed we were young again. Laughing and naked we ran across a
smooth lawn and dived clean and sure
into a clear green pool.

I ride that charged imagery all the time now,
when my dancer's feet no longer point, and my leg no longer rises into
arabesques.

I ride it over the worry we share over our shared money, the
spot of your skin, or the fall we both fear,
out of this life together.

Ride it hard over the phone call to a new doctor hinting
something amiss in the brain of our young son, hating when the young are touched!

See your hand now as you reach for me? See your
lined face against my arm? A landscape of the
investment we made in us.

Come, love, tonight we swim again.

## *Etruscan*

Ancient afternoon, a rustling in the Temple, and
then the scent of cypress stealing along the tiles
under curtain swelling with air warmed over waves on the
Mediterranean.

They lie, arms thrown against the Azul mosaic, living frescos,
their
robes lifted for love,
both givers and given, they are quiet now in
the wash of fading sunlight across column,
floor and face.

Their pleasure knows no bounds here among
this moment caught,
faceted and radiant. Moments focused in
a single glimpse of light slipping now
behind the horizon.

## *Spanish Dancing*

His mouth opens to the caves of Andalusia, singing of
gypsies in wagons blistered and wandering.
He sings the song of riding rootless over
centuries, of darkness rising
and falling, falling into a light pooled now
beneath a woman's feet. Her feet heavy,
ingrained deep into the floor of this wooden stage and all
the others coming before
this night and after.

Palmas suspend yielding in the air, signaling
pulse and tempo into her waiting arm.
He wails his words, and she is an answer,
receptive and charged, her wrists turning, her
waist twisting slowly, she is formed from the
voice, poured from the song.

And as she moves, their story is told; *remember, remember,*
they say as her heels stamp notes
of sweaty victory against the earth, releasing primal code
through spotlight, floor, crust, and core until a swelling
rises up, the air an orgasm suspended, and they are
home, these gypsies.

# *Vacation for Stanley Hall*

The jet touches down lightly, wafting in on an ocean breeze. Down into
L.A. and its manufactured ease,
he floats through this city both at home and removed. Removed
from needy students,
bitchy soloists,
thick-headed board members
at home in Austin, Texas with his past now
softened in reels of aging technicolor.

Here, past backlots and sound stages where hidden in the wings hang
the ghost steps of hundreds of old dance routines
that still run up and down his synapses when he watches 'Silk Stocking,'
'Gentlemen Prefer Blondes,'
'Guys and Dolls.'
Cyd Charisse was "mahvelous, dahling," but oh how they loved Marilyn.

They sit schmoozing in his friend's apartment grown shabby and spare. two old
queens letting down the hair. God! That hair,
an impossible brick red,
the other's, a shoe-dye black, a

white patch
where they forgot or didn't bother to look anymore.

They drink gin, smoke incessantly, "My dear, I never inhale,"
escaping
the present which can't help but pale
against that clubby inner circle of their past, Juliet
Prouse, "what a bitch!"
Jack Cole, "true genius."
Bogart, "a nice man."
They re-taste the time-worn fullness of old news.

A peculiar light settles quietly in the room, they
sit, spent, stare, and all too soon
the thread is lost, connective tissue torn.
Smoke clears,
memory collapses,
glasses sweat
rings on the table that swells between them into half a continent of time.

Departure is awkward, the breeze no longer lifts or sustains.
His legs stiffen with effort as he hurries for his plane back
to the suburban studio afterlife.
Don't touch the girls. Don't
get close to the boys.
Don't bruise the fleshy egos of their parents.
Until the next suggestion of, no, a statement for, escape.

# *About the Author*

Lisa Smith, MFA, retired Professor of Practice, Director of Dance, Department of Theatre and Dance, University of Texas at El Paso for 20 years. She was honored by the Outstanding Faculty Awarded in the Arts. She has been teaching dance and directing dance programs and dance companies for almost 45 years. Her experience spans the elite pre-professional dance schools, community dance programs for disadvantaged children, NEA-sponsored residencies, and higher education. She has taught students from age 3 to 63 in a variety of workshops, classes, and conferences, and she has been an active choreographer of recitals, musicals, operas, and both ballet and contemporary dance productions throughout her career. She has written a number of essays, reviews, poems, and a chapter from a book titled "The Dance Experiment: Insight into History, Cultures, and Creativity" by Myron Nadel. She had a stroke, and since that went on to teach the Aphasia and brain injury.

www.ingramcontent.com/pod-product-compliance
Lightning Source LLC
Chambersburg PA
CBHW020939090426
42736CB00010B/1202